People From Many Places

Copyright © by Harcourt, Inc.

All rights reserved. No part of this publication may be reproduced or transmitted in any form or by any means, electronic or mechanical, including photocopy, recording, or any information storage and retrieval system, without permission in writing from the publisher.

Requests for permission to make copies of any part of the work should be addressed to School Permissions and Copyrights, Harcourt, Inc., 6277 Sea Harbor Drive, Orlando, Florida 32887-6777. Fax: 407-345-2418.

HARCOURT and the Harcourt Logo are trademarks of Harcourt, Inc., registered in the United States of America and/or other jurisdictions.

Printed in Mexico

ISBN-13: 978-0-15-352803-3
ISBN-10: 0-15-352803-6

If you have received these materials as examination copies free of charge, Harcourt School Publishers retains title to the materials and they may not be resold. Resale of examination copies is strictly prohibited and is illegal.

Possession of this publication in print format does not entitle users to convert this publication, or any portion of it, into electronic format.

3 4 5 6 7 8 9 10   050   11 10 09 08 07

Visit *The Learning Site!* **www.harcourtschool.com**

Moving to New Places

READ TO FIND OUT **Why do people move to new places?**

People have come to the United States for many years. They come for new opportunities. An **opportunity** is a chance to have a better life. Some come for freedom. Some come for jobs. Some come for school. Some come to leave danger behind.

Young children come to the United States with their families.

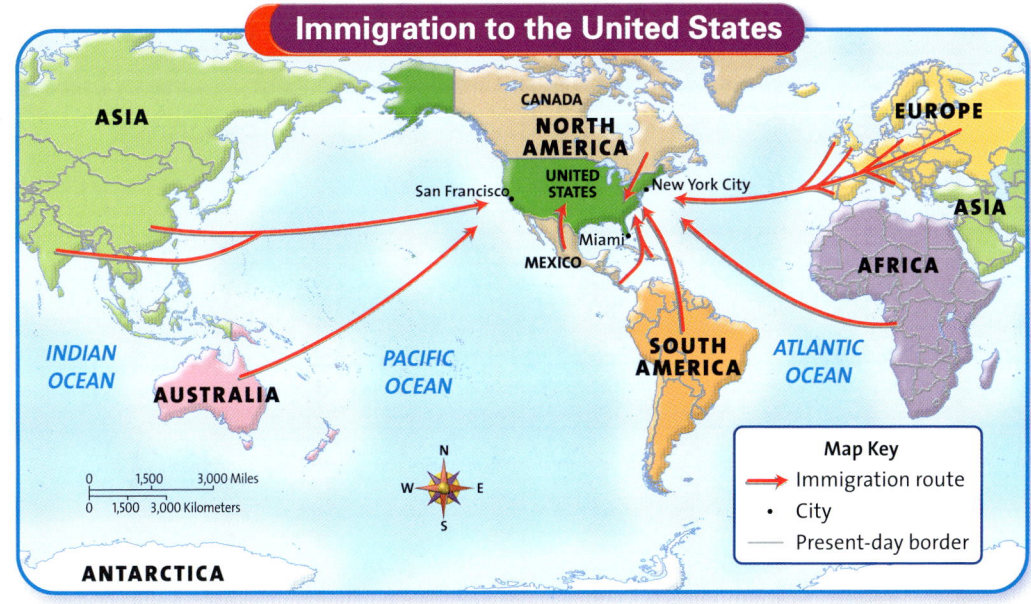

People come from all over the world.

In the past, many people came to our country. They faced many problems. Most did not speak English. They had a hard time getting jobs. They had little money. They lived in small places.

People still come to this country. Some come from Asia and Latin America.

READING CHECK CAUSE AND EFFECT **Why do people move to new places?**

Sharing Cultures

READ TO FIND OUT How do different groups in the United States share their cultures?

People bring their own cultures to a new country. Different cultures make places **diverse**, or different. They give people the chance to learn about other cultures.

Games can be shared.

Food is part of a person's culture.

A big city has many people. Some groups of people share the same language and culture. These groups have their own traditions. A **tradition** is something that is passed on to others.

People can share their traditions with others. Families share their kinds of food. Children might share their games.

READING CHECK **MAIN IDEA AND DETAILS** How do different groups in the United States share their cultures?

Our American Heritage

READ TO FIND OUT What makes up our American heritage?

People in the United States share many beliefs. This is our American heritage. Landmarks are part of our heritage. A **landmark** is an important natural or human feature. The Statue of Liberty is one. It is a symbol of freedom.

The Statue of Liberty is a well-known American landmark.

Independence Day is a holiday.

Holidays are another part of our heritage. A **holiday** is a special day. Holidays help people remember a person or an event. One holiday is Independence Day. We use this day to remember the beginning of the United States.

READING CHECK **MAIN IDEA AND DETAILS** **What makes up our American heritage?**

7

Expressions of Culture

READ TO FIND OUT **How do people share their culture?**

People can share their culture through stories. A **myth** is one kind of story. It is made up. It explains something about the world. Cultures around the world have myths. Other made-up stories are about real people or events.

Stories are one way to share culture.

Synagogue

Church

People can share their culture through dance and music, too. They sing special songs.

Religion is another way to share culture. Each religion has different traditions.

READING CHECK **MAIN IDEA AND DETAILS** How do people share their culture?

9

Holidays and Traditions

READ TO FIND OUT What are some holidays and traditions?

Holidays are important to many cultures. One holiday is Cinco de Mayo. This is a holiday in Mexico. People fill their homes with lights. They eat special foods.

Another holiday is Kwanzaa. It celebrates African American family life.

Cinco de Mayo is celebrated with Mexican dance and music.

People celebrate New Year's Eve together.

New Year's Eve is another holiday. People have fun on this special day. In New York City, people celebrate together. In Belgium, children give notes to their parents.

Chinese New Year is also celebrated. In China, families have a special dinner. Chinese children are given money for good luck.

READING CHECK **MAIN IDEA AND DETAILS** What are some holidays and traditions?

Cultures of the World

READ TO FIND OUT How are cultures around the world different?

Many cultures in the world are alike. But they are also different. People can speak different languages. They can eat different foods.

People around the world are proud of their own cultures. The clothes people wear show their pride.

These drummers and singers are at a festival in Ethiopia.

Buildings can show things about a culture, too. Some old buildings in Japan were made of wood. They had many openings. Air could move through the rooms. This shows that nature was an important part of the culture.

READING CHECK **COMPARE AND CONTRAST How are cultures around the world different?**

Japanese house

Vocabulary Power

Activity 1

Match each word to its meaning.

opportunity   diverse

tradition   holiday

landmark   myth

1. a chance for a better life
2. something passed on to others
3. a story to explain something about the world
4. a special day
5. an important natural or human feature
6. different

Activity 2

Look at the list of vocabulary words. Categorize the words in a chart like the one below. Then use a dictionary to learn the definitions of the words you do not know.

opportunity	landmark	festival
prejudice	statue	cultural identity
migrate	holiday	legend
custom	literature	folk song
diverse	myth	worship
ethnic group	fable	tradition
multicultural	folktale	

	I Know	Sounds Familiar	Don't Know
tradition			✓
diverse		✓	
myth	✓		

Review

Cause and Effect Why do people come to the United States?

Vocabulary
1. What is one **tradition** in your family?

Recall
2. What is Kwanzaa?
3. How do Chinese families celebrate Chinese New Year?
4. What is one American landmark?

Critical Thinking
5. Why are myths important?

Activity

Draw a Picture Draw a picture of a holiday you like. Write a sentence about the picture. Tell why you like the holiday.

Photo credits Front Cover Jeff Greenburg/Photo Edit; 2 Bettmann/CORBIS; 4 Jeff Greenberg/Courtesy of Convention & Visitors Bureau of Greater Cleveland; 5 John Kuntz/The Plain Dealer; 6 John Wang/Getty Images; 7 Ariel Skelley/CORBIS; 8 Syracuse Newspapers/John Berry/The Image Works; 9 (tl) age fotostock/SuperStock; (br) Spotworks, Inc; 10 AP Photo/Kevork Djansezian; 11 AP Photo/Julie Jacobson; 12 Dave Bartruff/Corbis; 13 Akira Kaede/Getty Images